At the Edge of the Pond

For
Stephen Alan Trimble

First Edition

Library of Congress Cataloging-in-Publication Data
Dewey, Jennifer.
    At the edge of the pond.

    Summary: Explores the levels of life in a pond from the muddy shore to the murky bottom.
    1. Pond ecology—Juvenile literature.   [1. Pond ecology.   2. Ecology]   I. Title.
QH541.5.P63D48   1987   574.5'26322   86-27417
ISBN 0-316-18208-7

Designed by Trisha Hanlon

WOR
Published simultaneously in Canada
by Little, Brown and Company (Canada) Limited

Printed in the United States of America

At the Edge of the Pond

Jennifer Owings Dewey

Little, Brown and Company
Boston   Toronto

Daybreak

Daybreak
at the edge of a pond.

Sunlight streams down.
The sun's warmth stirs creatures of the pond
to hunger and activity.
Life fills the air.
Life fills the water.
Chirps, buzzes, hums, croaks, and splashes — sounds
from the pond grow lusty and strong
as the day begins.

What makes a buzzing noise?
What splashes?
What scurries in the grass?
What croaks?

Insect wings buzz in flight.
A turtle falls into the water with a splash.
A water shrew races in the grass along the edge
where land and water meet.
A frog croaks.

Brightly lit surface water blinks and prickles
with swimming whirligig beetles, water striders,
and water measurers.

In plant-tangled shallows, yellow-and-black water snakes
squeeze through narrow openings between stems.
On the oozy pond bottom
a dragonfly nymph searches hungrily
for something to eat.
A giant water beetle leaves an air bubble floating
on the surface after it dives.

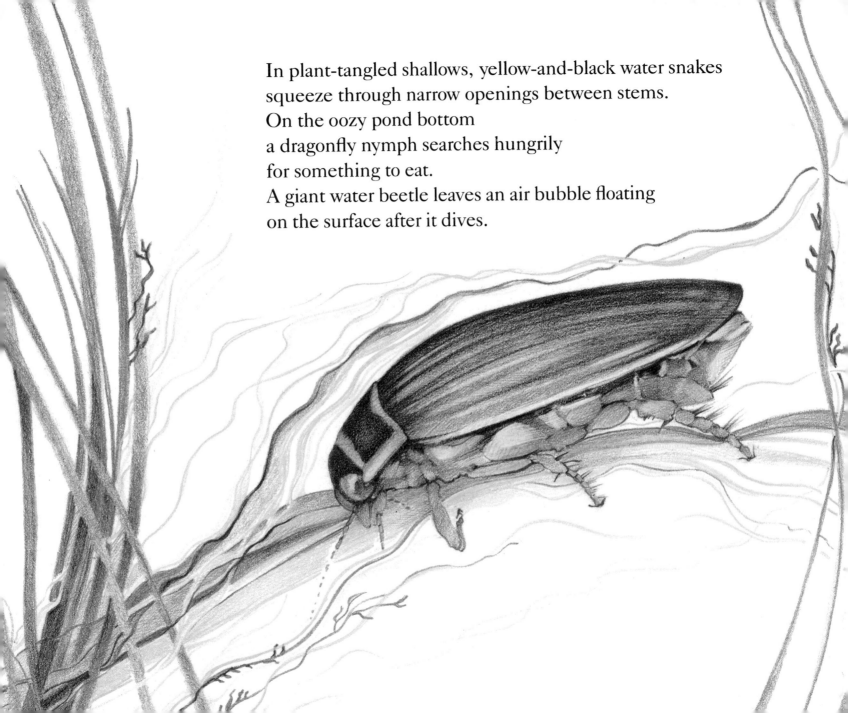

The watery world of the pond
is transformed by morning light.
Green plant cells respond to sunlight,
turning it into food, into energy.
All life depends on energy — energy from the sun.
Green plants make sugar molecules out of sunlight,
water, and air — the first link in the earth's
food chain.
All green plants, and some bacteria,
produce food,
from the smallest to the biggest,
from microscopic green algae
to flowering pond lilies and cattails.

A pond is almost all water,
shallow, still, and fresh.
Pond life wakes up to the new day
in countless different ways.

Crustaceans, smaller than a drop of water,
crawl about on the surface.
Dobsonflies and mayflies take to the air,
spinning territorial circles over the pond.
A fisher spider hides in a thicket of weeds
at water's edge.
Frogs sit on lily pads and logs
like frog statues, taking in the light.

The turtle seeks warmth, too.
It scrambles up onto a log, the same log
it climbs up on every day.

Big or little,
visible or invisible,
turtle, frog, nymph, or mosquito — all life
dwelling in the pond
begins the exercise of a new day
when the sun rises.

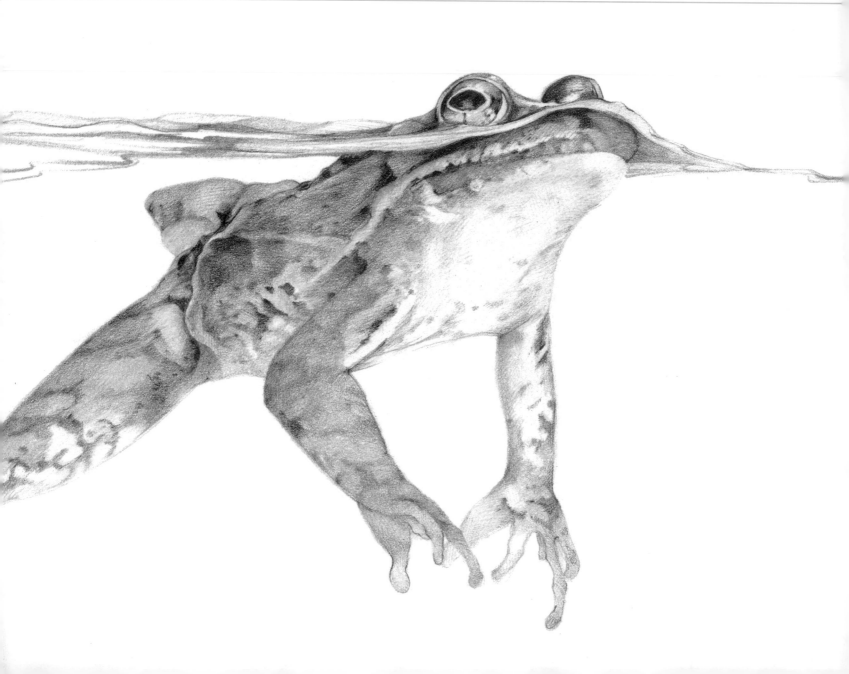

The Surface of the Pond

Sometimes the surface of a pond is glassy and smooth.
Sometimes wind makes the water ripple,
and sunlight dances on the ripples.
What moves there?
What swims?

A water strider slips between two stems
and skims out over the water's mirror surface,
its six legs reflected beneath it.

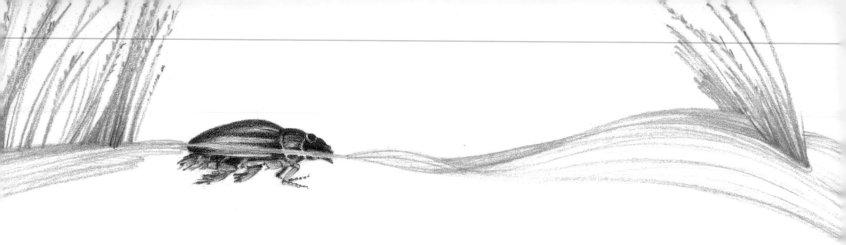

A whirligig beetle gyrates its way through a forest of stems,
spinning a dizzy track across the surface.
A water flea, propelling itself with feathery antennae,
feeds on grains of pollen caught in the surface film.
A pickerel frog plops into the water,
breaking the surface and making waves.

The waves surprise the water flea, tossing it into the air
to land helplessly on the surface film.
Trapped.
The whirligig, a fast and tireless swimmer,
reaches the water flea in an instant and makes a meal of it.
For some the surface is home,
for others a death trap.

The surface of a pond is a line, an edge between two worlds.

The claws of the water scavenger beetle repel water,
so it can walk upside down under the surface film.
The fisher spider's body has thousands of hairs all over it.
Each hair acts as a sense organ — the spider reacts
if one is touched.
The fisher spider is supported by the surface film,
a thin but dense layer of water molecules.

Water molecules attract each other, creating surface tension.
Surface tension makes the water surface firm,
firm but elastic,
a floor to some, a ceiling to others.

Half above the water, half below,
the whirligig beetle swims.
Its waterproof back, curved like a shell,
lustrous and black, glistens in the sun.
The only pond beetle able to swim through the surface film,
it travels in groups of five or six,
or sometimes swims alone.
It grips prey with long front legs,
and pushes against the water with mid and hind legs
fringed with hair.
The whirligig keeps an eye on both worlds.
The beetle's eyes are divided into two distinct parts,
one to see above the water, one to see below.
When alarmed, the beetle dives — a bubble of air
trapped under its wing covers serves as an underwater air supply.
Using this bubble, the beetle can stay submerged for hours.
When the bubble collapses, the beetle rises to the surface
to breathe, to trap another bubble
under its wing covers.

With a single, silken line, a lifeline,
the fisher spider skates across the water surface,
capturing insects snared in the surface film.
Its legs span four inches.
Underneath the spider's feet the water bends
but does not break.
To go under water the spider pulls itself down,
under a floating leaf or branch.
Air trapped in the hairs of its body forms a coating.
The spider breathes this air when it dives.
At night the fisher spider's eight eyes glow,
green and gleaming, in the reeds
at the edge of the pond.

Pond animals traveling from water to air,
or from air to water,
pass through the surface film.
For some it is a hazardous journey:
the film can grip and hold
a tiny animal.

In the pond
the balance between life and death
is a fine line.

A prickle of movement, a speck on the water,
a bubble bursting — mosquito pupae wriggle out of sight
under floating twigs and leaves.
The tiny, gray, oblong shapes
hang under the surface film from breathing tubes
made of fine hairs.

The pupae, called wrigglers, have bristles
on their faces that sweep particles of food
into their mouths.
Danger lurks everywhere.
Wrigglers are eaten by frogs and salamanders,
water snakes and giant water beetles.
If nothing eats them, they grow, and they molt,
and they go on molting
until the final molt.
Front legs, hind legs, head, and chest,
all unfold out of the wriggler's last molt.
Sacs flattened along the wriggler's sides
fill out into wings.
The old skin falls away.
Steadying itself with a claw at the tip of each foot,
the new mosquito steps across the surface film.
Crawling slowly up a stem to dry off,
the mosquito's life under the surface film ends,
and a new life in the air begins.

The Shoreline

A splash, a guttural rumble,
peeps and raspy croaks,
high-pitched whistles spaced a second apart . . .
Pulses of sound fill the air — frog voices,
a mixture of frogs.
Green frogs, pickerel frogs,
grass frogs, and bullfrogs.
Shrill frog noise circles around the shore
of the pond.

The ground along the shore is spongy, squishy, and wet.
A water shrew, its belly empty and aching,
runs a zigzag path at shore's edge,
where land and water meet.

Stopping to investigate a leaf fragrant with rot,
the shrew uses its quivering, whiskered nose
to explore beneath it.
A many-legged centipede or a ripe earthworm
might be hidden there.
Nothing.
The shrew takes off again.
Frog croaks lift and fall in the air.

Concealed in clumps of tussock sedge near the shore,
frogs sit and call out in rhythmic,
patterned tones.

The full-throated croaking of the male frogs
attracts the females.
Their mating goes on for several days.
When it is over, masses of frogs' eggs float
in silvery, jelly-like rafts
on the surface of the water.

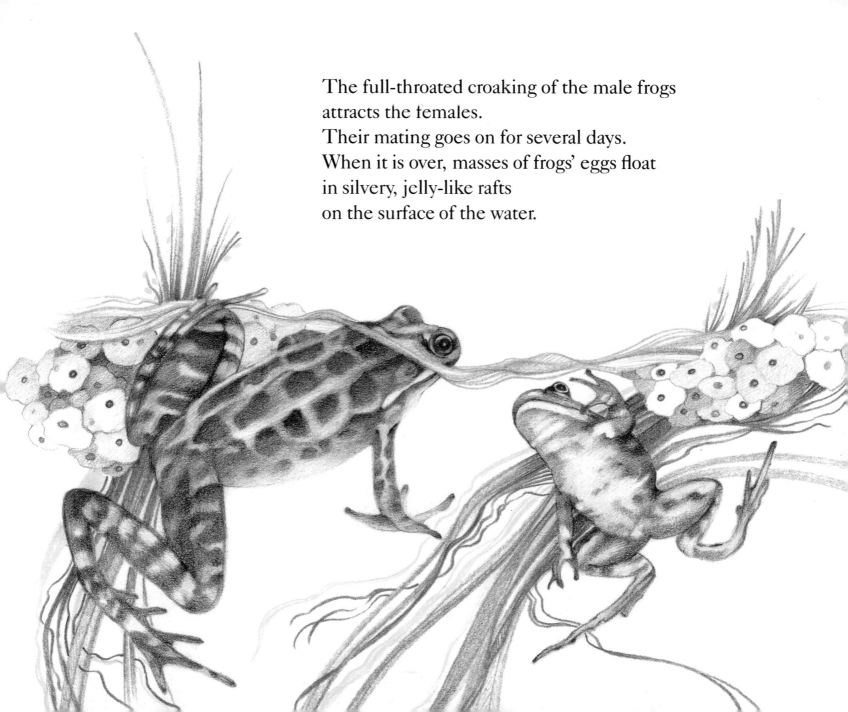

In two weeks tiny tadpoles, soon to be frogs,
hatch and enter the water.
Clusters of tadpoles, darting and wiggling,
are prey to dragonfly nymphs, fisher spiders, and water beetles.
Those not eaten grow quickly — in seven weeks they have legs
with webbed feet attached.
Beady eyes protrude above round frog snouts.
The tadpoles have lungs and breathe air.
Tails erode away, leaving recognizable frog bottoms.
When brand-new frogs hop out of the water
for the first time,
the transformation is complete.

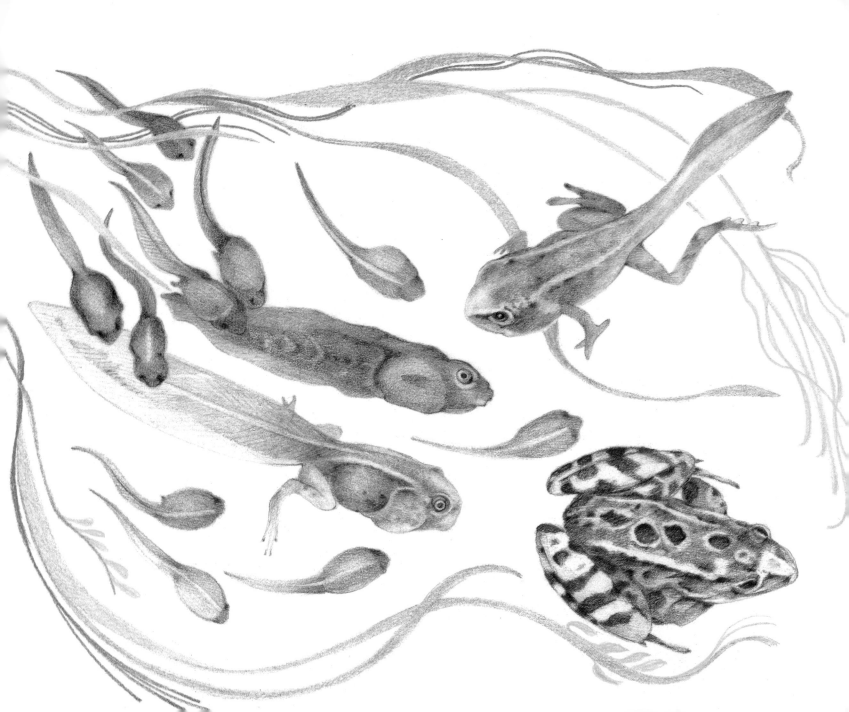

Trembling slightly, whiskers twitching,
the water shrew sits under an overhang of willow.
The shrew is still — still, at least, for a shrew.
Footprints etched in mud
show where the animal has scampered.
Dots of light flash from its eyes.
It begins to groom, rubbing its nose with its forepaws,
drawing back its upper lip to show rows of tiny, sharp teeth.
The shrew stops rubbing its nose.
Alert to something sensed, not seen,
the shrew is poised, ready to dive.

Water shrews live short, intense lives.
Owls eat them.
Raccoons eat them.
Often the small fires of their lives burn out
in their struggle to survive.

With a leap
and a squeak,
the shrew is gone.
Water droplets hang in the air,
a faint splash noise startles birds
in the willow up above.
The shrew vanishes through the surface of the water.

From the moment of the shrew's entry into the water,
countless bubbles of air trapped in its fur
sheathe it in silver.
Stiff hairs on its legs, feet, and toes
act as stabilizers, making the shrew
fast and efficient.

Flaps inside the shrew's ears fold down,
keeping out water.
The shrew sees poorly — it follows its nose.

Swimming close to shore, almost able to touch bottom,
the shrew shoots past water snakes, slithering and glassy
in the shallows.
It stops to nip at a tangle of waterweed.
A shred of this weed catches in the shrew's fur,
trailing behind it, a drapery of lacy green.
The shrew goes under, comes up,
goes under again.
It scatters a swarm of inky black tadpoles
hanging together in the water.
The clump of tadpoles turns into a hundred dancing shapes,
each separated from the other.

A water beetle is unaware the shrew is near.
Swimming around submerged leaves and stems,
working its way to the surface to breathe,
the beetle rises higher and higher.
Darting out of shadows cast by strands of weeds,
the shrew attacks in a single motion,
chomping through the insect's outer shell,
killing it instantly.

Twisting, weaving in the water, heading for dry land,
the shrew carries its victim clamped tightly
in its jaws.
The shrew will find a safe place on shore
to hide and to eat its meal.

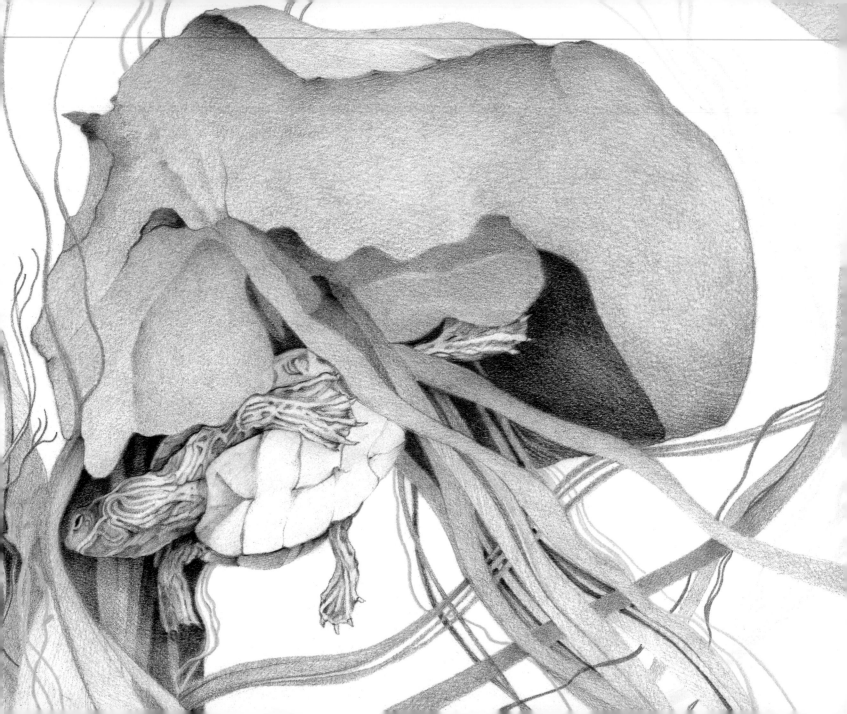

Deep Water

Flickering, silty sunlight, dark shadows,
tangled masses of waterweed,
sturdy water lily stalks —
the deep water world is a hidden world,
a place of diffused light
where the sun's rays do not penetrate far.

A giant water beetle, nearly two inches long,
sculls up through deep water.
Two back legs fringed with hair
beat together,
giving the beetle force and speed
in its swimming.
It stops swimming near the surface
and floats up the rest of the way.

Rear end up,
it rises to the underside of the surface film.
Two hairs at the tip of its abdomen
spread against the film.
Air enters the beetle's tissues
through tiny holes under the hairs.
The beetle breathes.

In an instant the beetle's air supply is restored.
It dives again.
Down into deep water the beetle swims.
Unseen in the water around it are countless numbers
of one-celled animals and plants,
the simplest life forms of all.
Free-swimming rotifers wheel up and down,
cilia drawing food particles into their mouths.
Green hydra snare and devour creatures smaller
than themselves, shooting harpoon-like filaments
from dangling tentacles.
Deep water life seethes and blooms.

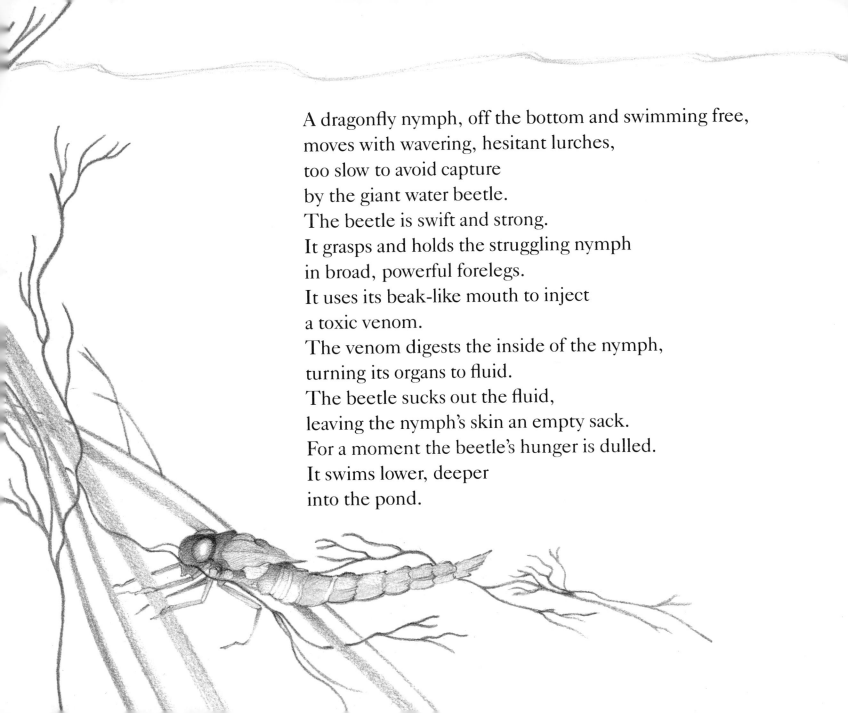

A dragonfly nymph, off the bottom and swimming free,
moves with wavering, hesitant lurches,
too slow to avoid capture
by the giant water beetle.
The beetle is swift and strong.
It grasps and holds the struggling nymph
in broad, powerful forelegs.
It uses its beak-like mouth to inject
a toxic venom.
The venom digests the inside of the nymph,
turning its organs to fluid.
The beetle sucks out the fluid,
leaving the nymph's skin an empty sack.
For a moment the beetle's hunger is dulled.
It swims lower, deeper
into the pond.

Water lily grows up through deep water,
its roots embedded in bottom mud.
Water lily leaves spread on the surface,
leaf-faces to the light.
Pickerel frogs, the sharks of the pond,
hide in deep shadows under lily pads.

Hiding under a lily pad, in dim, mottled light,
a pickerel guards its territory.
No other frogs may invade,
no other frogs may use the pickerel's hunting grounds.
Blotched markings on the frog's back side
blend with sun-speckled, dappled shadows
under floating leaves and stems.
The pickerel is streamlined, fierce, and fast.
It shreds prey with rows of sharp, pointed teeth.

Swerving right and left,
the glossy, oval shape of the giant water beetle
beats up through the water.

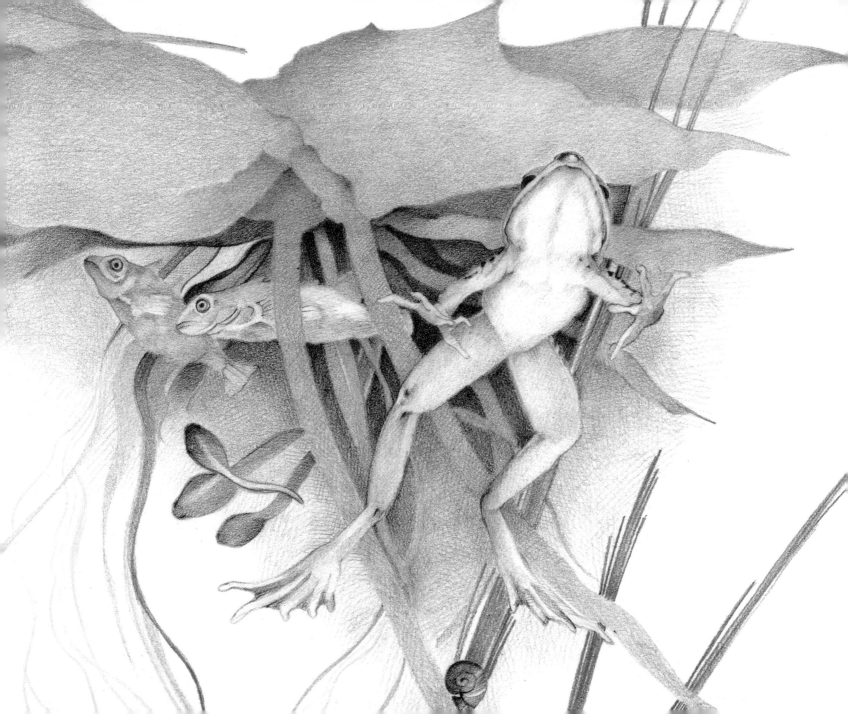

The pickerel frog is still,
waiting.

The beetle's path, and the hunger of the pickerel,
would have spelled disaster for the beetle,
had not a merganser chosen this moment
to swim out into the pond.
Feathers tight and oiled,
wings pressed to its sides,
the merganser swims on sunlit ripples
on the surface of the water.

The merganser dives.
Bubbles stream in its wake.
The duck's course through the water
forces the beetle to change direction.
It finds a new way
to get to the surface.

The beetle lives another day.
The pickerel still waits.

The Pond Bottom

Twigs snapping, splintering, and breaking
startle a pond turtle resting on a log.
Tumbling into the water with a soft, slapping noise,
the turtle half swims, half floats
to the bottom of the pond.
Sinking lower and lower,
the turtle falls through shimmery, sun-bright colors
to faded, twilight shadows.

It lands on the bottom, nose first.
Poking with a bony beak, scraping with clawed forelegs,
it nuzzles at leaf fragments and feeds.
The turtle moves without effort, safe on the pond bottom.
It passes colonies of red worms
living upside down in their burrows in the mud.
Spiny, creeping crayfish scavenge on the bottom,
five pairs of walking legs carrying each one along.
Clams lie half-buried in the mud,
fringed gill openings releasing coils of bubbles.

Water lice dance among the bubbles,
like puppets on invisible strings.

Invisible, too, are bacteria
living in pond bottom ooze.
Tiny animals sprawl on top of the ooze,
while the bacteria live under it.
Light is scarce on pond bottoms.
In these dim, shadowy places,
animals move slowly, and hide easily.
Bottom dwellers need less light, and less air,
than animals elsewhere in the pond.

Swiping at the bottom with a clawed foreleg,
the turtle creates a small storm of rotting plant remains.
Swirling around the turtle, spreading through the water,
the cloud of debris throws a one-eyed copepod off balance.
The copepod, swimming sideways in the water,
is blinded and stunned. It collapses
and sinks to the bottom.

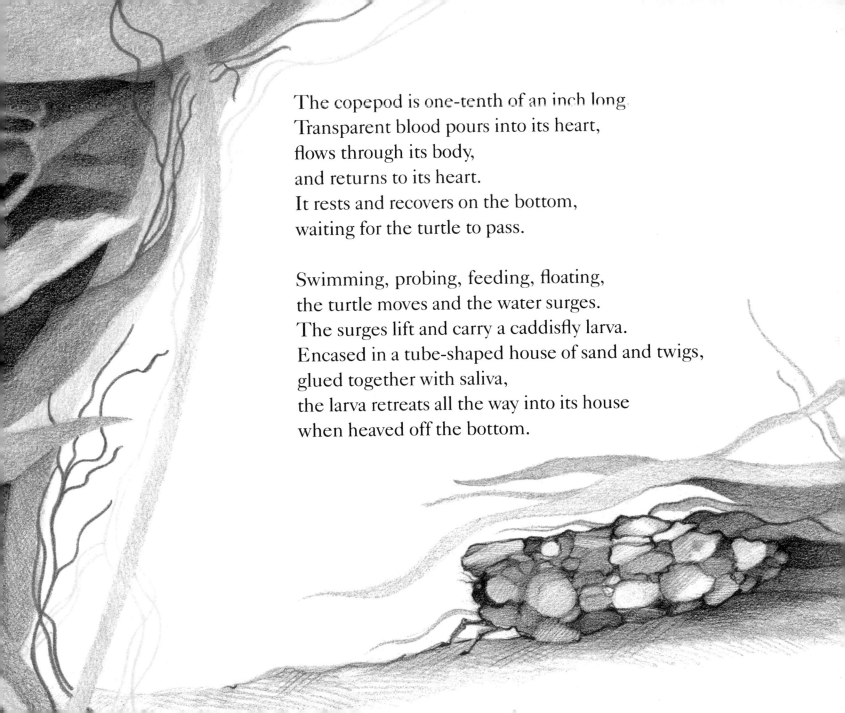

The copepod is one-tenth of an inch long.
Transparent blood pours into its heart,
flows through its body,
and returns to its heart.
It rests and recovers on the bottom,
waiting for the turtle to pass.

Swimming, probing, feeding, floating,
the turtle moves and the water surges.
The surges lift and carry a caddisfly larva.
Encased in a tube-shaped house of sand and twigs,
glued together with saliva,
the larva retreats all the way into its house
when heaved off the bottom.

The turtle moves away into murky, glimmering shadows.
In its wake a bead-like head appears.
Forelegs poke out.
The caddisfly crawls across the bottom,
dragging its case behind.

It does not crawl far.
Suddenly a dragonfly nymph lunges into view,
rolling out of fluid darkness.
It surprises the caddisfly into retreat.
The caddisfly vanishes into its mobile house.
Jerking, swimming, and crawling forward,
the dragonfly nymph is propelled by jets of water
squirted from its tail.
Huge eyes cover most of its head
and meet at the center of its brow.

Blending perfectly with the leaf-littered pond bottom,
the caddisfly is not seen by the nymph.
Not nimble, yet fearfully adept as a hunter,
the dragonfly nymph misses out
on this particular meal.

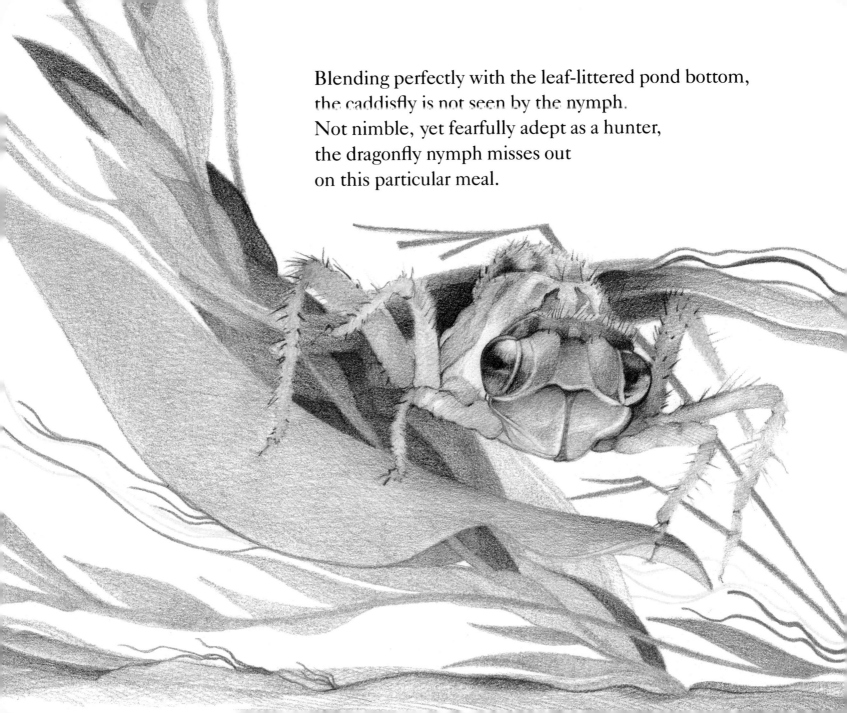

The turtle swims close by. It has circled back
toward where it first entered the water.
Curiosity, not hunger, draws the turtle to the nymph.
It nudges and pokes at the thick, segmented body.

The nymph's forelegs,
bunched against its head,
fly out in a single spasm of effort — an effort
to escape the probing and shoving of the turtle's beak.
The nymph lumbers off, a shudder passing through its body.
It moves with dumb, awkward movements,
yet is one of the pond's most feared predators.

The caddisfly emerges again—trembling a little
in waves of movement in the water surrounding it.
The dragonfly nymph has disappeared.
The caddisfly moves forward
and begins to feed.

Lifting off the bottom,
pushing against the water with webbed feet,
the turtle rises to the surface to breathe.
This dark, flattened shape moving up
through beams of silty sunlight leaves
trails of bubbles following behind.
The turtle vanishes.

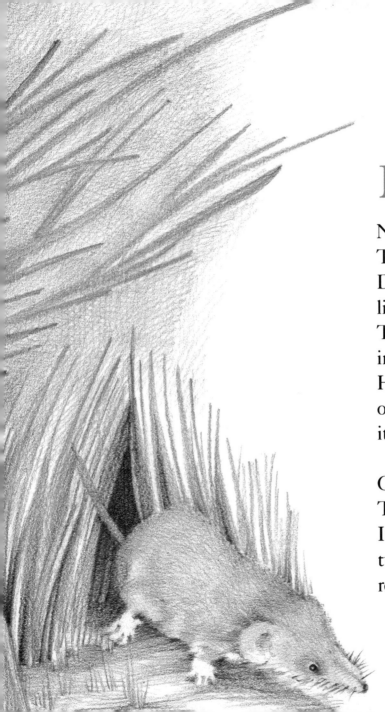

Nightfall

Nightfall.
The day ends when the sun goes down.
Darkness moves through the trees
like smoke.
The fisher spider's eight eyes flash green
in the reeds at water's edge.
Hunting at night, the spider launches
onto the surface film,
its line of silk strung out behind it.

Owls hoot.
The water shrew tries to hide from them.
It dashes up and down tunnels in the grass,
tunnels formed by the passage of countless
rodent feet.

The turtle hides, too,
for warmth and for safety.
It pushes itself into a space under a log,
a space just big enough for itself.

Night sounds are soft, indistinct, muffled.
The dragonfly nymph makes no sound
creeping across the bottom in the full darkness
of the night.

The pond will change again
at daybreak.
A pond is always changing
and never still.